Affirmations

Embrace Your Quirkiness

Destiny S. Harris

. . .

...

Copyright

Copyright © 2023 Destiny S. Harris.

Front cover image by Destiny S. Harris.

Book design by Destiny S. Harris.

First printing edition 2023.

www.destinyh.com

...

. . .

A Gift For You

Thank you for taking the time to read this book. As a token of my appreciation, here is a gift to you.

I give away free books daily. Here's how to get your free books today:

Step 1: Visit

amazon.com/author/destinyharris

Step 2: Filter books by "Price: Low to High"

Step 3: Download available free eBooks

. . .

...

Table of Contents

. . .

...

Quick Bit

Thank you for taking the time to read this book.

My hope is that you leave at least 1% better than before you read this book and walk away with at least one takeaway.

I'd like to graciously ask that you help me by leaving a <u>review</u> of this book; your feedback helps me write better books and helps others get a glimpse of the book.

With Kindness,
Destiny

. . .

. . .

#1 Uniqueness

I am unique, and I'm comfortable with it.

I love and enjoy being different.

I do not shy away from what makes me different.

I'm not trying to be like everyone else.

I embrace all the traits, characteristics, history, goals, and quirks that make me unique.

. . .

...

#2 Differences

I embrace others' differences.

I embrace my differences.

I am not an assimilator.

I stay open to how I evolve, no matter how different the evolution looks compared to others.

I am accepting and open-minded to everything that makes everyone unique.

. . .

. . .

#3 Strange

Being "strange" is a gift.

I never want to be "normal."

I'm gifted with strangeness.

I am confident and comfortable with who I am.

I am perfect the way I am, and that's all that matters.

. . .

. . .

#4 Separation

I do not look to befriend everyone. Nor do I seek everyone to befriend me.

Most importantly, I accept myself, the first criterion for others to accept me.

I am okay with having a mental separation from others who habitually assimilate with popular thought.

I accept my differences and focus on attracting others who vibe with my uniqueness.

I separate myself from others who misalign with who I am to protect my mental and emotional energy.

. . .

...

#5 Beautiful Acceptance

I love who I am and the person I'm evolving into.

I accept myself wholeheartedly.

I embrace the individual I am today and the individual I will be tomorrow.

I set aside abundant unconditional love for myself and others daily.

I am grateful for who I am now.

. . .

...

#6 Unwavering

I do not change who I am to satisfy others.

I stay true to my colors, values, and personality.

I am comfortable being different from others.

I stay open to the differences of others to explore, learn, and understand people, but I do not sacrifice myself in the process unless there is a better truth for me to adopt.

I am confident with who I am and secure in my identity.

. . .

. . .

#7 Loving The Self

I love and am loving towards myself.

I appreciate myself.

I embrace myself.

I am secure in myself.

I am kind to myself.

...

...

#8 No Impressing

My goal is never to impress others but to be myself.

I have nothing to prove to anyone except myself.

I am comfortable presenting who I am today to others.

I am the best representation of myself now.

Who I am today is more than enough.

. . .

. . .

#9 Self Accept

I accept myself.

I am open-minded to all of what makes me who I am.

I appreciate the magnitude of my strangeness.

I admire the quirkiness of my being.

I am comfortable representing my whole self to the world.

. . .

. . .

#10 100%

I am 100% comfortable in my skin.

I am 100% comfortable in my strange being.

I am 100% comfortable in my quirkiness.

I am 100% comfortable with my uniqueness.

I am 100% comfortable with my differences
from the world around me.

...

...

Thank You For Reading

Thank you for reading this book.

Stay loved, blessed, lucky, favored, aware, joyous, and committed to bettering yourself.

. . .

. . .

The End.

...

. . .

About Destiny S. Harris

Destiny S. Harris' goal is to positively inspire, cultivate, elevate, and educate the minds of individuals across the globe through her writing.

Creating (whether books, courses, articles, poetry, or music) has always been Destiny's thing, not to mention health & fitness and all things entrepreneurial.

Destiny published her first book, "Beauty Secrets for Girls," at age 11 and her second book, "Don't Wait Until It's Too Late," at age 12.

Destiny obtained three degrees in Psychology, Political Science, & Women's Studies. She also started her own music teaching business at the age of 14, which she led for over ten years. In addition, she has been teaching academic, career, and personal development topics to thousands of students and readers since 2004.

Outside of writing, Destiny loves and enjoys a few other things: reading, weightlifting, walking, biking, traveling, football, dogs, animals, food, classic movies, mountain and ocean views, sleeping, plants, and nature.

Check out her work, leave a review, share your thoughts with your friends and family, and be a part of a movement: helping people learn and grow through means of self-education (books).

<u>Complete the Steps To Get Free eBooks:</u>

Step 1: Go to amazon.com/author/destinyharris

Step 2: Filter books by "Price: Low to High"

Step 3: Download available free books

...

. . .

Connect W/ Destiny S. Harris

Please reach out and stay in touch. Start a conversation today @ destinyh.com

. . .

. . .

Free Gifts!

Access courses & free eBooks at the link below:

destinyh.com

...

Please Leave A Review

If this book impacts you in some way, please let me know by dropping a review on it.

I write better books with **your** input.

...

Tell Me What You Want

I've written many books, but if you don't see what you're looking for or need, get in touch with me via my website, articles, comments, or reviews, and let me know what you're looking for so I can create it for you. I'm here to serve.

Destiny

. . .